WORLD PEACE

and
How to make it Happen

A Practical Guide
MONISH DHAWAN

DEDICATION

I accept my Divine Nature in all its glory and its meekness.

I Dedicate this Book to My Father Vinay Dhawan whose sacrifice of love (death) pushed all the rest of us in my family... towards asking Important Questions and finding their answers about life, My Mom Varsha Dhawan, My Sister Ruchira, My Brother Sandeep and My lovely Nephews without whom the world wouldn't be the same Ansh and Rohan, for Supporting me all through.

To my Visible Guides and Mentors: Patriji, Dr.Newton, Dr. Lakshmi, Leonard Orr.

To all my Invisible Guides and Masters.

To all my friends who have supported me in taking this cause forward.

To all of you who are going to take this Noble cause forward and turn it into a Reality.

Last but not at all the least... to the one and only without whom none of this would ever have been Possible 'Myself'.

FOREWORD

This Book has the Potential to Manifest the Dream Humanity has been Dreaming for Centuries, and also to show us that the time to Manifest it has arrived... The Dream to Live on a Earth that is Peaceful, where all the Human Race lives as one, in harmony with each other, understanding that we all are actually just walking each other home.

A Dream where the whole of Animal Kingdom feels safe and interacts with their human brothers and sisters with love and care and vice-versa.

A Dream where all the Plant Kingdom, the Forests, the Animal Kingdom and Natural Resources are respected by humans, and we learn to live in harmony with each of them.

This book has been written with the intention and understanding, that World Peace or the way I like to call it, Peaceful Earth, is indeed possible by 2020 and, to show you how simple it actually is ... Are you game?

Table of Contents

"The day science begins to study non-physical phenomena, it will make more progress in one decade than in all the previous centuries of its existence. To understand the true nature of the universe, one must think it terms of energy, frequency and vibration."

– Nikola Tesla

1. I M POSSIBLE

When man dares, God Helps – **Holy Quran**

What If I was to tell you... We can create a Peaceful Earth by 2020, there is a science and if we apply this science with a strategic plan, we can actually manifest a Peaceful Earth by 2020. Would you be interested in learning about that plan?

To ignite your interest further let me tell you... what I mean when I say 'Peaceful Earth':

Peaceful Earth = Peace for Humankind.
Which implies, we live in a war free world, a rape free world, a crime free world, a conflict free world... no, wait let me use the correct words.

A World where all the countries are friends with each other

A World where every woman, child and man are completely safe

A World where every human being has more than enough to eat, clothes to wear and a house they can call home
A World where every human being is healthy, wealthy, happy and wise.

That was about the human kind, but earth does not just consist of human beings, right…!

Peaceful Earth also = Peace for Animal Kingdom
Peaceful Earth also = Peace for Plants and Natural Resources

And Peaceful Earth also = Peace for every other Kingdom on Earth that we humans are probably not even aware of but who cohabit this earth along with us.

Sounds like a fairytale, an impossible mission?

Here, let me promise you something: By the time you reach the end of this book you will be convinced that, yes, this is possible.

Deal?

2. PEACEFUL EARTH

Even if your belief is the size of a mustard seed you can move the mountains - **The Bible**

Albert Einstein once said... We cannot resolve a problem from the same level of thinking that created it.

Similarly, the previous chapter and the creation of 'Peaceful Earth' seems impossible to us right now, because we are not yet exposed to the information that can actually help us create such a world, that too in such a short span of time.

I have travelled across the world and asked hundreds of random people the following question:

Do you want Peace on Earth?

Every single one of them answered... YES

But when I asked them: Do you think it is possible to create peace on earth?

Then I got varied responses, some said 'NO', some said 'I don't think so', some said 'impossible', some said 'I want it, but not everyone wants it' and some dared to say 'YES'!

To those who said 'YES' I asked: By when?

Some said 'maybe 100 years', some said '50 years', some said 'maybe 20 years' then I asked them ... How?

Nobody had any answer... they all went mute.

This is the exact reason we do not have Peace on Earth today, we all want peace but most of us do not believe that we can have peace, and those who would like to believe that there can be peace, have no idea on how to create peace.

Therefore, by the end of the day each and every one of us give ourselves some lame excuses, like, the world is so big, how can I make a difference, what will happen if only I want peace, everybody should want it, nobody cares, or simply blame the politicians and who ever we can.

But the actual Truth is that, we actually have no idea if it is possible at all, during the 16 – 20 years of our school and college life the information we have gathered, the news channels and the movies that we see, from where we form the idea of how the world is today, none of these places actually talk about it, in fact, all of these sources only make it harder for us to believe, that it can happen, because all of them are telling us that, the world is becoming worse day by day.

3. THE GOOD NEWS

As you Think & Feel... So it Happens – **Gita**

For centuries human beings have fought against every problem and hoped we will create peace after that, we are doing the same today, we have war against terrorism, we have war against cancer, we have war against hunger and so on and so forth.

Albert Einstein said: Insanity is doing the same thing again and again and expecting different results... aren't we as the whole human race following insanity?

Let me ask you one more question:
More than 210 governments in the world, countless NGOs, and God knows how many millions of people are involved in these wars...! Is there a single problem that we can say we have completely resolved? Even one problem? Okay, maybe one or two battles, we have managed to win, but have we won any war?

I do not want to be a pessimist here, I am just trying to say, maybe somewhere, we are making a fundamental mistake, maybe our approach to resolve the issue itself is somehow going wrong?

Thankfully, I am not the only one who is thinking this way, in fact there are many scientists and universities who have been asking these questions, and searching for a different approach to create permanent Peace on Earth.

The Good News is that the scientists have been successful in finding the way.

But before I tell you about the path that they have discovered, let me tell you about the fact that ever since this research has been in duration, it has generated many successful experiments, so far and is ongoing in action!

According to Scientist David Orme-Johnson Ph.D. there has been more than 50 experiments during the past 40 years, and all of these experiments have been published in scientific journals including the very prestigious 'The Journal of Conflict Resolution'.

At the end of this book there is a Link to a Document which shows the bibliography of all the researches that took place and where they were published. You are free to download it and look for yourself.

When I came across this research and its profound findings, the first question that I asked myself, why has none of the media covered it? Then I realized, one result was covered by media, but that was about it.

4. THE RESEARCH

Never doubt that a small group of thoughtful committed citizens can change the world; indeed, it is the only thing that ever has. -
Margaret Mead

In this chapter I will share with you a few researches, just to let you know how powerful this technology is and the reasons these Researches are Accepted by Independent Scholars as well.

The power of peace-creating groups to decrease warfare and terrorism has been tested repeatedly. The results produced by temporary peace-creating groups (lasting weeks or months) have been consistently positive—with *nearly immediate reductions in war deaths averaging better than 70%.* In addition, the one peace-creating assembly that lasted for several years was accompanied by *a history-transforming wave of peace* around the world.

Most of these studies have been carefully scrutinized by independent scholars, then accepted for publication in mainstream academic journals.

Research:
A day-by-day study of a two-month assembly in Israel during August and September of 1983 showed that, on days when the number of participants at a peace-creating assembly was high, the intensity of an ongoing war in neighbouring Lebanon decreased sharply. When the number of participants was high, *war deaths in Lebanon dropped by 76%.* (p<.0001). [The mathematical expression *p<.0001* indicates that, as a result of standard

mathematical analysis, the likelihood that this result could be attributed to chance variation in levels of fighting was less than 1 in 10,000.

This amounts to a much higher *confidence level* than what is typical in the social sciences.

The same study also demonstrated improvements in a wide variety of social indicators—including crime, traffic accidents, fires and the stock market.

These various measures ordinarily have no correlation (you can't predict the stock market by watching crime statistics, for example). The fact that they all improved together—in correlation with an increasing meditation attendance — strongly indicates that peace-creating assemblies radiate a generalized influence of harmony and coherence throughout society that can be measured in many different ways.

The figures above illustrates a highly statistically significant correlation between daily changes in attendance at this peace-creating assembly and the daily changes in a composite quality-of-life index that measured all the variables together—war, crime, fires, accidents and the stock market. The correlation is so strong it can be seen in the raw plot of the data—even without mathematical analysis.

This study was accepted for publication in the most highly regarded journal of peace studies (*Journal of Conflict Resolution* 32: 776-812, 1988).

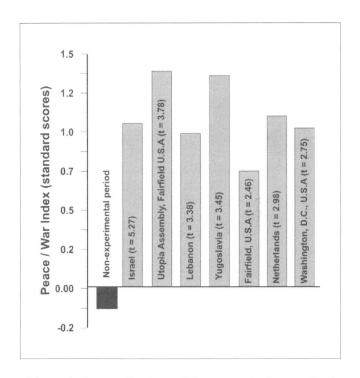

This study is a replication of the war-reducing results in Lebanon found in the previous study. This time the researchers looked at not just one peace-creating assembly, but seven consecutive assemblies (93 days altogether) over a two-year period during the peak of the nearly continuous Lebanon war. Some of these assemblies were relatively small but close by (one in Lebanon itself, and one in neighbouring Israel). Some of these assemblies were large (6,000-8,000) and distant (Holland and the United States).

By a ratio of size to distance, all of these assemblies were large enough, in theory, to affect the fighting. This study is especially significant because the ongoing warfare in Lebanon was a combination of conventional warfare, guerrilla warfare, and terrorism. As compared to all the other days in the 841-day study, during the 93 days of those peace-creating assemblies:

- war-related fatalities decreased by 71% (p < 10^{-10})
- war-related injuries fell by 68% (p < 10^{-6})
- the level of battles and other conflict dropped by 48% (p < 10^{-8})
- cooperation among antagonists increased by 66% (p < 10^{-6}).

These four results were combined into a composite Peace/War Index for the Lebanon War between June 1983 and August 1985 (see chart above). During each of the seven experimental periods, time series impact assessment analysis indicates significant progress towards peace.

Because the number of days in the study was so large, and a dramatic reduction of war was replicated seven consecutive times, *the likelihood that the combined results were due to chance is very nearly nonexistent —less than one part in 10^{-19} (p<.0000000000000000001.*

Making the peace-creating effect of group meditations the most rigorously established phenomenon in the history of the social sciences (Journal of Social Behaviour and Personality 17(1): 285–338, 2005).

Accepted by Independent Scholars:
Research studies investigating an idea like peace-creating groups—a concept that transcends the dominant materialist paradigm of modern science—must run a gauntlet of highly sceptical scholars.

For those unfamiliar with research procedures, the publication of a scientific study implies more than mere printing and distribution. Most research journals are refereed—distinguished experts in the field (*referees*, or *peer reviewers*) judge every submitted study. When a theory is new or particularly controversial, referees assess the studies more strictly. Acceptance for publication indicates that the studies have been judged by professional quality, worthy of attention by the wider community of academic experts.

By now peace-creating assemblies have been thoroughly field-tested in more than 50 demonstration projects, and most of these demonstrations have been covered in 23 academically published scientific studies. Here are some of the reasons why research on such an innovative topic has attained such frequent acceptance:

Repeated findings: The more frequently a theory has been tested, the more confidence scientists place in the results. Nearly all of the published research on peace-creating assemblies reports on either a number of separate assemblies in one study (replication), or one assembly that increases and decreases in attendance many times (de facto replication).

Strong correlations: Scientists accept that cigarettes cause cancer because repeated studies show that the correlation between smoking and cancer is strong. In the same way, studies on peace-creating assemblies have been accepted for publication because they show strong correlation between peace-creating groups and reduced crime, warfare and terrorism.

Lead-lag analysis: In studies where attendance at the group of peace-creating experts varies over time, it is often possible for direct assessments causation through lead-lag (or transfer function) analysis. Such analysis shows what changes primary : peace-creating attendance or social violence (crime, war, etc.). In all the studies in which such lead-lag analysis has been possible, the evidence show that the meditation attendance changes first, and the measures of social violence soon after. This strongly indicates a causal role for peace-creating groups, and has been decisive in the publication of key studies.

Ruling out alternate explanations: To be convincing, any study must rule out alternate possible explanations for the results. Since violent crime, for instance, typically increases as daily temperature increases, researchers must account for temperature changes in their analysis. In these studies, researchers have carefully demonstrated that alternate possible explanations—such as weather, regular weekly, monthly or seasonal changes, changes in police patrolling, etc.—cannot account for the evidence.

Studies easily replicable (use of open public data): One of the most convincing aspects of this research is the open, public nature of the evidence. A lot of sociological research is based on privately gathered data that other scientists can only accept on faith. The research on peace-creating groups, on the other hand, is doubly public:

1. The dates and approximate attendance of most peace-creating assemblies are available in contemporaneous newspaper accounts.
2. Statistics on social violence, including crime, accidents, warfare, terrorism, etc., are available to any researcher with access to public records.

This public nature of the evidence means that any given study is replicable by other researchers—a strong safeguard for scientific accuracy.

Would you be Interested in learning more in detail about these researches and how to apply this science in bringing peace to yourself and your family I recommend that you

Sign up for free on www.mypeacefulearth.com and explore the video section filled with hundreds of similar research videos.

5. UNDERSTANDING THE RESEARCH

A revolution is coming – a revolution which will be peaceful if we are wise enough; compassionate if we care enough; successful if we are fortunate enough – but a revolution which is coming whether we want it or not. We can affect its character; we cannot alter its inevitability. **– Robert. F. Kennedy**

The Research has 2 sides to it...

1. The Research says that when a Group of people equal to the size of 1% of the world's population Intend for 'Peaceful Earth' or 'World Peace' or 'Peace on Earth'. The power of this intention will then have its effect on the entire population of the earth. The one percent of the world's population today is approx 71 million people.

2. However the second and more exciting part of the research is: It tells us that, if the people meditating can come together physically and intend for 'Peaceful Earth' in a meditative state of mind, we will need just about the square root of one percent of the world's population which would, for today's population make approximately 10,000 (taking the higher side)

Yes it is an astounding finding, Just 10,000 people coming together physically and meditating with a Single intention 'Peaceful Earth', can magnify the peace vibrations for the whole earth.

Which means the number of people required to create a "Peaceful Earth" is less than the number of people of an attending audience that watch any popular football or a cricket match in any stadium around the world, because the average capacity of any football or cricket stadium is anywhere between 20,000 to 60,000.

In India itself we have more than 120 Stadiums which have a seating capacity from 10,000 – 68,000. And around the world we have around 12,000 stadiums in 224 countries.

You might be wondering, why am I talking about stadiums suddenly? Well you will understand when you read the next chapter.

6. THE PLAN

Those who have the privilege to know, have the duty to act. **– Albert Einstein**

This Chapter is the MOST IMPORTANT chapter of this book, because in this chapter we bring the Utopian Idea of Peace and convert it in to a practically applicable plan…

Now that we have established the fact, that creating personal Peace collectively does create a 'Peaceful Earth'.

Let us have a look at the strategy, when applied collectively can create a 'Peaceful Earth' on or before the year 2020.

Let us review the Science:
1. We need a minimum of 10,000 people to collectively and physically come together and intend for 'Peaceful Earth' in a meditative state of mind.

2. We need this to happen every day of the year to 'Magnify the Peace Field'.

Yes that is all we need.

Since the benefit of the meditation of these 10,000+ people is going to reach all the people on earth.

Why don't we all share the responsibility and create 365 groups of 10,000+ people each? Yes, 365 cities, one city for each day of the year.

This way, each group takes the responsibility to 'Magnify the Peace Field' for one day per year.

Not one group alone gets the pressure of saving the world and everybody gets to participate, as well as take the responsibility of creating a 'Peaceful Earth' Peacefully.

The best part of this, is the fact that, the larger the number of participants per day, the merrier.

Now what would these 10,000+ people do the rest of the year?

Practice... Yes practice Meditation in small or large groups, in our offices or schools or colleges for at least 15 minutes a day. This practice will help us keep our personal and social life Peaceful.

At the same time 364 X 10,000+ people will also be contributing in 'Magnifying the Peace Field' along with that one city designated for that day. We all support each other, we all contribute and Magnify Peace together.

7. MEDITATION & DOUBTS

You cannot travel on the path until you become the path itself. -
Buddha

In This Chapter let us tackle the first challenge at hand, let us start by learning Meditation ourselves first, just in case you are not already a practitioner.

Before Teaching How to Meditate, let me break some of the most common beliefs and misconceptions people carry with them when it comes to Meditation.

1. **Meditation is very difficult:** contrary to common belief, Meditation is actually easy and very simple and can be done any time of the day.

2. **I cannot concentrate or Focus thereby meditation is not for me:** Wrong, Meditation is a practice of which, one of the side effects is increase in your focus and concentration levels, which means if you cannot focus or concentrate you need to meditate even more. I have witnessed when students who do not accomplish well in schools or colleges and are taught meditation, and their scores increase to a remarkable level.

3. **Meditation is for old people:** again wrong, the youngest age any one can be taught meditation is 3 years, yes that is how old one needs to be to learn meditation.

4. **I cannot sit in a complete lotus position, forget the lotus position I can't even sit straight:** One need not sit in a lotus position to meditate you can sit in any comfortable posture, be it on a chair, a sofa or on the floor, just make sure you cross your legs and clasp your hands, if you cannot sit straight that is not a problem either, you can take a back rest, just make sure you do not rest your head.

5. **I am too materialistic, Meditation will turn me into a saint and I will lose interest in my family and life:** A huge misconception, I have been teaching meditation since the year 2000 and till this date I haven't seen anybody running away from their life and family, in fact I have only seen people make their relationship better, accomplish their 'materialistic' goals which they never thought were possible before. Meditation only increases your energy to live life fully and your capacity to believe in yourself.

6. **I do not have time for Meditation:** This is a Big one, a lot of people simply do not commit to meditation because they feel they do not have time, however, Meditating in the morning makes your whole day go slower and many people say they actually get more done and feel more productive after meditation. Because meditation helps improve focus and lowers stress, you actually can fit more in if you take the time out to practice.

8. BENEFITS OF MEDITATION

Meditation makes the entire nervous system go into a field of coherence. **- Deepak Chopra**

Though there are endless lists of benefits you receive, as a gift for consistently meditating in your life, here, I will list the most common benefits regular meditators report.

Speedy healing of diseases of all sorts: people have healed from sinus to cancer with the help of meditation. There are more than 6000 scientific studies conducted world over on how people have healed their diseases through regular practice of meditation.

Memory power in students is increased: More and more schools and colleges have included meditation as a part of their daily activities and are finding great results.

Productivity of employees is increased: Slowly but steadily corporate around the world are opening up to the Idea of introducing meditation to their employees as they are finding increased productivity in their employees performance, and more harmony among the employees in the office environment.

Interpersonal relationships become better: Couples and families have reported time and again that their understanding levels have improved tremendously, since they started practicing meditation.

More and more celebrities and famous personalities are coming out in public today and vouching to meditation for their personal growth and success.

Wasteful Habits die naturally: Regular meditators have reported that they have been able to gain control over their wasteful habits like over eating, over sleeping, lethargy, smoking, over drinking etc., more effortlessly with the help of meditation.

Clarity in purpose of life: People who practice Meditation have reported that they have been able to gain more clarity in understanding their purpose of life.

Intuition power increased: People who meditate regularly, report that their ability to discern between right and wrong has sharpened, they are able to use this power while making important decisions at a job or in business.

9. TYPES OF MEDITATION

Mindfulness is often spoken of as the heart of Buddhist meditation. It's not about Buddhism, but about paying attention. That's what all meditation is, no matter what tradition or particular technique is used. - **Jon Kabat-Zinn**

Now that we know there are so many benefits to Meditation, let us look in to the Types and science of Meditation.

Some meditation teachers emphasize that meditation is a state of mind involving awareness and acceptance, and can thus be done at any time in the midst of any activity. There are countless forms of meditation, but most fall into three or four general categories: concentrative, open awareness, and guided – as well as the broadly defined practice of mindfulness.

Concentrative Meditation: In this practice the objective is to cultivate a single-pointed attention on some object, such as a sound, an image, the breath, or a flame. Through the training of consistently returning to the object of focus, the mind develops the capacity to remain calm, stabilized, and grounded. Many Western meditation teachers start beginners with this practice, most commonly focusing on the breath. In some advanced practices, states of bliss may be reached. The most well-known and researched form of the concentrative type in the West is Transcendental Meditation (TM).

Open Awareness The objective of these forms of meditative practices is to open the mind into a panoramic awareness of whatever is happening without a specific focus. Often this awareness is compared to the spacious sky or a river with objects floating by. The capacity to be present with whatever arises is developed through this practice. The Zen sitting practice zazen, or shikantaza, is an example of this form of meditation practiced in the West.

Mindfulness: The most popular, widely adapted, and widely researched meditation technique in the West is known as mindfulness meditation, which is a combination of concentration and open awareness. Mindfulness is found in many contemplative traditions, but is most often identified with the Theravadan Buddhist practice of vipassana, or "insight meditation." The practitioner focuses on an object, such as the breath, bodily sensations, thoughts, feelings, or sounds. The focus is not as narrow as in concentrative meditation, for there is a simultaneous awareness of other phenomena. This mindfulness practice is often extended to daily actions, such as eating, walking, driving, or housework. The contemporary Western adaptation is typically removed from the rigorous contemplative training method of empirical introspection traditionally associated with Buddhism, which has as its objective the development of equanimity and clarity of perception.

Guided Meditation: All forms of meditation can be guided, and many are often practiced with recorded or in-person guidance at first, and then later with decreasing need for explicit guidance. In one form, called guided imagery, the practitioner follows auditory guidance from a teacher or recording that elicits certain images, affirmations, states (such as peacefulness), or imagined desired experiences. Guided imagery is popular in the West to facilitate health and well-being and is often used to rehearse successful outcomes of procedures, such as surgery or an athletic performance.

Now that you know about the Various kinds of Meditation Techniques let's dive in to learning one of them, and the one I have chosen to share here, is called Mindfulness or Breath Awareness Meditation.

10.HOW TO MEDITATE

Half an hour's meditation each day is essential, except when you are busy. Then a full hour is needed. - **Saint Francis de Sales**

In Mindfulness or Breath Awareness Meditation, the mind's attention should constantly be on the breathing.

The task at hand is conscious observation of the breathing. No mantra is to be chanted and no form of any deity is to be entertained in the mind. No pranayama practices like kumbhaka (holding the breath) should be attempted.

Any comfortable seating posture can be assumed. The posture should be as comfortable as possible. The hands should be clasped, and the eyes should be closed. The crux of the matter is to resist the routine wanderings of the mind. Thoughts should be cut right away, as and when they arise.

Process of Meditation:
-- BE CALM.
-- BE STILL.
-- SIT IN A RELAXED POSTURE.

Inhale Slowly. Exhale Slowly
Let your breath be a rhythm of calm
your breath is a rhythm of calm
follow your breath

Be Calm
--   Use your mind to follow your breathing

--   in...out...in...out
--   that is all

Be Still
--   Be as one with your breathing-energy
--   Immerse yourself in your breathing-energy

The **Breath Awareness Meditation** is so simple and easy. It can be done by anyone, of any age, at any time and at any place.

Meditate for a minimum time in minutes as is your age in years. (For e.g., Meditate twenty minutes if your age is twenty years) Meditation should be done regularly.

To be able to taste all the benefits of meditation, one needs to Meditate at least forty days continuously, after which the decision to continue or dis-continue can be taken.

11. MAKING IT HAPPEN

Knowing is not enough, we must Apply...
Willing is not enough, We must Do **– Bruce Lee**

Now that we know how to meditate we have taken care of the first challenge, Let us now look in to how to tackle the second challenge.

"Making the local group in your city to collaborate and come together for one day each year."

Yes, the research is there, the science is proven; I am considering that you are willing to participate and practice Meditation for yourself, your family and to our earth's benefit.

What can you do now?

I have realized that many great ideas die off because people keep waiting for someone to come forward and take the first step, that is why I have taken the first step for our Earth by developing a social networking site which is specifically designed to help all the interested people to come together on a single platform and collaborate locally as well as internationally.

All you need to do is Sign up on www.mypeacefulearth.com in this website, people signing up from the same city are automatically added to a common local group, so that you can meet other likeminded people from your city and collaborate.

And when you reach 10,000 in your group, you can collectively announce a date for the Peace festival in your city.

This website also maintains a Common Calendar for 365 cities.

Other than that the following are the basic steps you can take...

1. Start Meditating yourself first, if possible in a group, for a minimum of 15 minutes a day.

2. Gift this book to the Dean of your school/ college or your organizations HR Manager/Managing Director; they will be able to help you form that group in your organization, as group Meditation for 15 minutes will create a peaceful environment in the organization as well. Ask them to experiment for at least 40 days and see the benefits for themselves...

3. In today's world we get so much over load of information, which is not necessarily always useful, but this overload of information makes us forget as to what is important, therefore I recommend that you keep visiting the video section of the website to remind yourself of this profound science, so that you can use it for your personal benefit, more sharply... remember Peaceful Hearts Create Peaceful Earth, Your Personal Peace is of utmost importance for 'Peaceful Earth'.

4. Buy five extra copies of this book and challenge five people to read this book within a month, if everyone who buys this book creates this

challenge we will be able to reach our desired target of 1% of the world population within 9 Months, Yes in 9 months we would reach 71 million people. All you need to do is make sure your 5 friends read the book.

12. Survival tips till we reach 'Peaceful Earth'

Four Steps one needs to follow to stay on the path of self-realisation, 1. Meditate every day 2. Read recommended books/ videos 3. Meet likeminded people regularly 4. Authentically practice them all –
Monish Dhawan

How to Deal with Constant Negativity of the world we already come across in our daily life?

We are all aware of the increasing negative hype all over the world. Therefore it becomes very important for us to have information on how to deal with this negativity so that it doesn't affect us and at the same time, also realize that collectively, we can do something to create a more positive environment around us.

How to **act positively** when you come across negative news-

1. Avoid excessive/repeated exposure to negative news

When you watch or read negative news, you feel emotions such as fear, anger, depression, hopelessness etc., which are unknowingly sent out into the universe. These play their part in creating our reality. Therefore, avoid repeated exposure to any kind of negative news. This way, you also avoid negative emotions which have the power to manifest themselves in you if you focus on them for too long.

Thought Creates Reality

We all know that our thoughts create reality. We have to be very careful of what we think, speak and discuss with others, be completely aware, and choose positive thoughts in order to create a positive environment.

2. Be aware and avoid fear/anger/depression programming

Do not forward mails or messages that encourage anger and hatred, or those with pictures of dead bodies, blood and other such images. All these add to fear/anger/depression programming leading to the creation of a mass destructive events.

Many Masters have said, "What we focus on expands. Focused consciousness creates reality." Therefore, let's choose to focus, i.e. think, talk and act, on only positive things like peace, love, joy, harmony etc.

3. Meditate immediately

As soon as you come across negative news, sit and meditate immediately with the intention of 'Peaceful Earth'. Imagine the power of millions of people Magnifying Peace vibrations, as a reaction to negative news that they come across!

4. Group Meditation

The energy in group Meditation is magnified many times more than individual Meditation.

An Experiment done in Washington DC:

For two months 4000 people were Meditating for a few hours a day, they were able to bring the crime rate of a city down by 25%, imagine the kind of peace vibrations we will be creating when millions of people meditate for 15 minutes every day with one single Intention.

Let us all contribute towards a 'Peaceful Earth' by Meditating twice a day for a minimum of fifteen minutes, one fifteen minute period at your home and a second period at your workplace, school or college.

If any personal or (inter)national negative incident occurs, you can invite people for silent group Meditations.

Participation in at least one group Meditation per day helps us stay positive and peaceful for the whole day.

13. TIME FOR ACTION

It Does not matter to me how much you know, what matters to me is how much of what you know, have you applied. **– Krishna to Arjuna in Gita.**

In this Chapter I am Going to attempt a step which is considered the most difficult thing in the entire world, that is asking someone to actually do something practical, and I hope you will be kind to me in making this attempt of mine a success by applying it.

When we look at the ocean, it looks very large and unfathomable but if we look at it closely, even the ocean is the combination of small little water droplets, similarly "Peaceful Earth" is the ocean, and each and every one of us is a droplet.

By now if you have reached a point where you agree that "Peaceful Earth" can be created, Now is the time to take action in that direction.

Mahatma Gandhi said: even though the step you take might seem very insignificant, it is still very important that you take it.

So at this point I would request you to do the following steps... now... yes I mean NOW:

1. Grab your phone or your computer, connect to the internet and go to www.mypeacefulearth.com and signup for free now, you just need to give your name, email and city... and I would push you a little again to grab

that phone of yours or your computer and do it now, as this is literally the first step you can take towards "Peaceful Earth" remember every drop counts, it might seem like an insignificant step as of now but let me tell you, it is one of the most important steps to create "Peaceful Earth", please do it now, keep this book aside and sign up on www.mypeacefulearth.com Now.

Thank You :-)

After that...

2. Log in to your email account and Write an Email to at least five or more friends, and recommend them to read this book. The book is available on amazon at this link: www.amazon.com/dp/B00SNUN9HU/

Consider this: If we start with 100 readers and each one of us, who reads the book, sends this email to five of their friends and they read the book and duplicate the process of sending emails to five of their friends and this process duplicates itself once every Month, we will be able to reach our target of 1% of world's population in exactly 9 Months, isn't that amazing!

Dear friend please do your Part Now. Small drops when collected together make the big oceans, every drop counts.

There is a possibility that you are thinking 10,000 people in my city, that is a big number... let's diagnose it, Yes if you live in a small village it might be true, but for a city with the population of a million plus 10,000 is just 1% of its population, the city I live in has a population of 7 million.

Wait let me break down the number 10,000 for you:
100 students from 100 colleges makes 10,000 or

100 employees from 100 companies makes 10,000 or

1000 employees from 10 companies makes 10,000.

Now the number 10,000 is seemingly simple right?

Let me make it even simpler: Let us say 10 people take the responsibility of reaching 10 schools/colleges or offices each in your city, after doing that you have reached 10,000.

Or

100 people reach out to 1 school/college or office per head.

The reason I am doing this is, until we all come to the point of believability, having the information and the precise plan will not work out, because we will not move a finger to make it happen if we do not believe in its possibility.

Even after reading the book and going through all the research, it will end up remaining a good nice Idea, as it remained for our ancestors and their ancestors... they all wanted Peace, just the way we do, but until we believe in its possibility, we will not move and make things happen.

Secondly we also need to understand that You have reached to a point of believing "yes Peaceful Earth is indeed possible" only after going through the book and its research, without this, world peace would still be a "nice old lady" idea, meaningless, that is the same process these 10,000+ people also need to go through, which is why I ask you to spread the word about the book, because without awareness and education of magnifying peace, we cannot expect appropriate action out of any one.

Remember Awareness and Education about "Peaceful Earth" is the first step.

I am doing all I can, but this is not possible without your Support... Please Signup on www.mypeacefulearth.com Now.

And if possible gift this book to five of your friends with a promise that they will read it within a month. You can choose to buy five more copies or just lend your copy.

14. Coming Together... Going the Extra Mile

If you want to go fast, go alone... If you want to go far, go together. - **African Proverb**

I might have thought of the Plan and the Strategy, but without your support and involvement this Idea will never happen, thereby I invite you, to come together and let us all make this dream a reality.

Let us create a Peaceful Earth... Peacefully, on or before 2020.

Now that we are aware of the basic steps everyone needs to take, here are a few extra steps you can take, to speed up the process of making this dream a reality.

1. After awareness and education... language is the most important challenge, which we need to overcome to make this message reach far and wide, therefore If you are a translator, and would like to translate this book into your language please email me immediately: peacefulearthfoundation@gmail.com
2. If you own a website please put this book on for sale on your website
3. In your Organization... Encourage competitions like: What will a 'Peaceful Earth' look like? More number of people imagining about a 'Peaceful Earth' strengthens the Vision and the Intention. It can be Essay writing, Drawing, Photography or a

Filmmaking Contest. Upload the results of the Competition to www.mypeacefulearth.com

4. If you are a filmmaker, insert the Idea of 'Magnifying Peace' and how it works, somewhere in your films, make short films or feature length films about the same.

5. If you are a Song Writer/Singer, Write/Sing more songs on creating Peace.

6. If you are in a position where you can make decisions, make a decision to educate your organization and everyone involved in it about the power of 'Magnifying Peace', it will help you create more Positivity and Peace in your organization as well.

7. If you are a Director or Producer and is touched by this knowledge, get in touch with me, I have an Idea to make a Docu-movie about the same and spread the message.

8. If you are in to Media, write about the Possibility of 'Magnifying Peace' let people know about this book.

9. If you are a film star or an influential personality, please stand up for this cause,go public.

10. If you know a famous personality, gift them this book and persuade them to read it.

11. If you are a Blogger, write about this Book, help this book reach more and more people.

12. If you are a Digital Marketer, use your knowledge to make this book reach more and more people.

13. If you are a Web Designer, help us improve our website.

14. If you have received this book for free, I recommend you to please go to http://www.amazon.com/dp/B00SNUN9HU/ and buy more copies of this book and ask your friends to do the same, all the money generated

from selling this book will go towards maintaining our website and creating a Documentary about Peaceful Earth to spread the word even clearer and faster. The more money you would want to donate ... the more books you will order.

15. Sign this petition here so that the government bodies also take this topic seriously, the more signatures, the more seriously the governments will take it: http://www.mypeacefulearth.com/petition/12/petitioning-presidents-prime-m

15. VIDEOS

Most of the things that you have read in this book are available in Video Format, you can see those Videos here all these videos are available on www.mypeacefulearth.com

Dr. John Hagelin Explaining about the Science:

http://www.mypeacefulearth.com/videos/1/12/course-one-peace-is-possible-par

http://www.mypeacefulearth.com/videos/1/13/can-group-meditation-create-peac

The Rice Experiment and Water Crystals Videos, Power of our Thoughts on the world around us:

http://www.mypeacefulearth.com/videos/1/16/course-one-part-four-rice-experi

http://www.mypeacefulearth.com/videos/1/15/course-one-part-three-water-has

Video by Institute of Heartmath on creating personal, social and global coherence:

http://www.mypeacefulearth.com/videos/1/37/course-one-part-six-individual-c

Scientist Gregg Braden Explaining the Science of Peace in Depth... Must Watch Videos:

http://www.mypeacefulearth.com/videos/1/109/gregg-braden-language-of-the-div

http://www.mypeacefulearth.com/videos/1/108/greg-braden-language-of-divine-m

How to Meditate and many questions about Meditation answered:

http://www.mypeacefulearth.com/videos/1/102/meditation-in-english-course-thr

Six Thousand Scientific researches about the benefits of meditation:

http://www.mypeacefulearth.com/videos/1/49/6000-researches-on-meditation-an

The Power of Intention Explained by Dr.Wayne Dyer

http://www.mypeacefulearth.com/videos/1/38/course-five-power-of-intenton

For 100's of more Videos
Visit www.mypeacefulearth.com

16. RESOURCES

Other Organizations working for the same cause directly or indirectly, you can also join them.

www.mypeacefulearth.com

http://permanentpeace.org/

http://www.heartmath.org

http://www.glcoherence.org

http://globalpeaceproject.net/

www.unify.org

http://1giantmind.org

http://www.worldpeacemeditation.org

http://bethepeace.com

http://www.medmob.org

http://www.gaiafield.net

http://www.earthdance.org

http://www.doasone.org

http://theshiftnetwork.com

http://summit.summerofpeace.net

http://pathwaystopeace.org

http://www.peaceripples.com

http://www.peaceoneday.org

http://compassiongames.org

http://www.intuition-in-service.org

http://sydneypeacedayfestival.com

http://www.lovesilence.com

http://www.themindfulbrain.net

http://gaiaminute.com

www.pssmovement.org

Disclaimer: I am not associated with any of the organizations or the scientists mentioned in this book (other than www.mypeacefulearth.com)I might have some friends in some of the organizations, though I would love to have friends in all of the above organizations, I do not own any of the videos which are shared in this book, they are all the properties of their respectful owners. I do not get any financial benefit from any of the websites mentioned above, I am sharing their details only because I feel they are doing great work and need applauds for their work.

If you would like your website to be on this list or delete your website from this list, please email me and I will add or delete it, in the next version of this book. peacefulearthfoundation@gmail.com

LINKS AND RESOURCES:

Download Word document, exclusive list of 60 research and review papers on 51 studies on the 'Maharishi Effect' (name given to this Phenomenon):

http://www.truthabouttm.org/documentFiles/20.doc

A PDF that shows summary of 503 researches on TM can be seen here:

http://www.truthabouttm.org/utility/showDocumentFile/?objectID=61

Website of Dr.John Hagelin Pioneer in this Research Work

http://www.hagelin.org/

Case Studies: http://globalpeaceproject.net/proven-results/case-studies/

Chapter 4 Research Source:
http://permanentpeace.org/

Chapter 9 : Sources : http://www.noetic.org/

How to Meditate: Source : www.pssmovement.org

No of Stadiums: Source :
http://www.worldstadiums.com/

RECOMMENDED BOOKS
AVAILABLE ON AMAZON:

1. The Intention Experiment by Lynne Mc Taggart

2. The Bond by Lynne Mc Taggart

3. The Field by Lynne Mc Taggart
4. E-Squared by Pam Grout

5. The Power of Intention by Dr. Wayne W. Dyer

6. The Isaiah Effect by Gregg Braden

7. Secrets to the Lost Mode of Prayer by Gregg Braden

8. The Divine Matrix by Gregg Braden

9. The God Code by Gregg Braden

10. The Science of Miracles by Gregg Braden

11. The Biology of Belief by Dr. Bruce Lipton

12. Complete set of 5 Volumes of Scientific Research on TM by Dr. David W. Orme-Johnson
13. The Hidden Messages in Water by Masaru Emoto

14. <u>The Miracle of Water by Masaru Emoto</u>

15. <u>Love Thyself by Masaru Emoto</u>

16. <u>The Healing Power of Water by Masaru Emoto</u>

17. <u>The Secret Life of Water by Masaru Emoto</u>

18. <u>You can Heal Your Life by Louise L. Hay</u>

19. <u>Your Body's Telling You: Love Yourself! : The Most Complete Book on understanding Health by Lise Bourbeau</u>

20. <u>Constant Craving: What Your Food Cravings Mean and How to Overcome Them by Doreen Virtue</u>

I Will Keep Adding to the List of Recommended books on Various Topics on our website
 www.mypeacefulearth.com

GRATITUDE

I would like to thank you all for taking the time in reading this book, watching the videos and helping in spreading the word.

I thank you from the bottom of my heart for helping in the creation of a 'Peaceful Earth'.

Remember if we all do our small part, the big thing will automatically happen.

3 simple steps:
1. 15 minutes group intention Meditation every day, after signing upon www.mypeacefulearth.com
2. Once a year mass group intention Meditation in your city
3. Spread the word(Email to 5 or more friends)

I WILL LEAVE YOU WITH THE VISIONS I SEE IN MY MEDITATIONS:

I See Millions of people Meditating together for 'Peaceful Earth', I See stadiums filled with people Meditating for 'Peaceful Earth', I See cities declaring a public holiday on their day of Peace Festival and all the stadiums, school and college grounds and public places like parks flooded with people, all of them Meditating for 'Peaceful Earth'.

I See Masses realizing the power within not only to magnify peace but also using the same power to fulfill their dreams and achieving success in their respective fields.

I See People becoming more healthy, self-responsible and happy

I See happiness, harmony and understanding among communities growing.

I See Meditation becoming a part of every corporate office, school and college, educating the students, on the science of 'Magnifying Peace' and applying it every day.

I See more and more moviemakers creating movies in many languages, getting inspired from this science and showing it in their movies.

Please share your, Meditation experiences on www.mypeacefulearth.com and be an inspiration to others.

Thank You for Making Earth so Peaceful.

ABOUT THE AUTHOR

Monish Dhawan

Monish Dhawan is an Author, Past Life Regression Therapist, Rebirthing Specialist, Inner-child facilitator, Spiritual counsellor, Speaker and a Visionary.

He has been Practicing Meditation and Teaching it since the year 2000.

His Vision is to Create a 'Peaceful Earth' on or before 2020, and he firmly believes that it is possible, this book is his attempt in making it happen.

He resides in Hyderabad, India but keeps travelling around the world.

You can reach him on www.mypeacefulearth.com or learn more about him and his work on www.monishdhawan.com

His Facebook ID:
www.fb.com/monishdhawan

Follow him on Twitter:
www.twitter.com/monish04

Alternatively Join the Movement on
Official Website: www.mypeacefulearth.com

like us on Facebook:
https://www.facebook.com/mypeacefulearthdotcom
Follow us on Twitter: www.twitter.com/mpeacefulearth

CAN I ASK A FAVOUR

If you enjoyed this book, found it useful or otherwise, then I'd really appreciate it if you would post a short review on Amazon / Create Space. I do read all the reviews personally.

Reviews also help other people make the decision whether to buy the book or not faster.

If you'd like to leave a review then please visit the link below:

http://www.amazon.com/dp/B00SNUN9HU/

Thank You for your support! ☺

Printed in Great Britain
by Amazon.co.uk, Ltd.,
Marston Gate.